MW01037427

REALLY BAD

Dad
Jokes

More than 400 Unbearable,
Groan-inducing Wisecracks
Sure to Make You the
Funniest Father With a Quip

—— Joe Kerz ——

Racehorse Publishing

Racehorse Publishing books may be purchased in bulk at special discounts for sales promotion, corporate gifts, fund-raising, or educational purposes. Special editions can also be created to specifications. For details, contact the Special Sales Department, Skyhorse Publishing, 307 West 36th Street, 11th Floor, New York, NY 10018 or info@skyhorsepublishing.com.

Racehorse Publishing™ is a pending trademark of Skyhorse Publishing, Inc.®, a Delaware corporation.

Visit our website at www.skyhorsepublishing.com.

10 9 8 7 6 5 4

Library of Congress Cataloging-in-Publication Data is available on file.

Cover illustration credit: Getty Images
Interior art credit: iStockphoto/Getty Images

ISBN: 978-1-63158-513-5
E-Book ISBN: 978-1-63158-515-9

Printed in China

INTRODUCTION

Fatherhood is never perfect. Try as you might to be there for your kids, you won't always succeed. However, they can always count on you to be there with the dad's most useful tool: the Dad Joke! The Dad Joke can always be used to embarrass and antagonize your children, eliciting the classic eye-roll, face-palm, and the occasional exclamation of *"DAD!"*—after all, isn't it a dad's main purpose in life to torment their children with puns in public?

Whether you're an expert pun-maker or a novice, you'll never run out of embarrassing riddles and puns with *Really Bad Dad Jokes*! This compendium of the most groan-worthy jokes and one-liners will be sure to

induce the reactions that you live for (even though they make your children die a little inside). Be prepared for any and every situation with a handy quip. Passing by a graveyard? I bet people are just *dying* to get in! Having pizza for dinner? Never mind . . . those jokes are just too *cheesy*. You'll never run out of opportunities to make your family wish they'd just left you at home!

So, grab your goggles and swim trunks and dive on into this book that's perfect for any father, young or old! You'll learn everything you need to know about mastering the art of the Dad Joke and unleashing your bad humor upon your family and the world. This may be the most important book you read all year because, after all, Dad Jokes are no laughing matter!

JOKES

1

DID YOU HEAR ABOUT THE RESTAURANT ON THE MOON?

Great food; no atmosphere.

2.

WHAT DO YOU CALL A FAKE NOODLE?

An impasta.

3.

How many apples grow on a tree?

All of them.

4.

Want to hear a joke about paper?

Never mind, it's tearable.

5.

I just watched a program about beavers.

It was the best dam program I've ever seen.

3

6.

What's the difference between a well-dressed man on a bicycle and a poorly dressed man on a unicycle?

Attire.

7.

How does a penguin build its house?

Igloos it together.

8.

SON: Dad, did you get a haircut?
DAD: No, I got them all cut.

9.

What do you call a Mexican
who has lost his car?

Carlos.

10.

Son: Dad, can you put my shoes on?
Dad: No, I don't think they'll fit me.

11.

Why did the scarecrow win an award?

Because he was outstanding in his field.

12.

WHY DON'T SKELETONS EVER GO TRICK OR TREATING?

Because they have no body to go with.

Daughter: I'll call you later.

Dad: Don't call me later, call me Dad.

14.

What do you call an elephant that doesn't matter?

An irrelephant.

15.

Want to hear a joke about construction?

I'm still working on it.

16.

What do you call cheese that isn't yours?

Nacho Cheese.

17.

WHY COULDN'T THE BICYCLE STAND UP BY ITSELF?

It was two tired.

18.

What did the grape do when he got stepped on?

He let out a little wine.

19.

I wouldn't buy anything with velcro.

It's a total rip-off.

20.

THE SHOVEL WAS A GROUND-BREAKING INVENTION.

21.

Daughter: Dad, can you put the cat out?

Dad: I didn't know it was on fire!

11

22.

This graveyard looks overcrowded. . . .

People must be dying to get in there.

23.

Cashier: Would you like your milk in a bag?
Dad: No, just leave it in the carton!

24.

5/4 OF PEOPLE ADMIT THAT THEY'RE BAD WITH FRACTIONS.

25.

Two goldfish are in a tank.

One says to the other, "Do you know how to drive this thing?"

26.

WHAT DO YOU CALL A MAN WITH A RUBBER TOE?

Roberto.

27.

What do you call a fat psychic?

A four-chin teller.

28.

I would avoid the sushi if I were you.

It's a little fishy.

29.

To the man in the wheelchair who stole my camouflage jacket . . . you can hide, but you can't run.

30.

THE ROTATION OF EARTH
REALLY MAKES MY DAY.

31.

I thought about going on an all-almond diet.

But that's just nuts.

32.

What's brown and sticky?

A stick.

33.

I've never gone to a gun range before.

I decided to give it a shot!

34.

Why do you never see elephants hiding in trees?

Because they're so good at it.

35.

Did you hear about the kidnapping at school?

It's fine, he woke up.

36.

A FURNITURE STORE KEEPS CALLING ME.

All I wanted was
one night stand.

37.

I used to work in a shoe recycling shop.

It was sole destroying.

38.

Did I tell you the time I fell in love during a backflip?

I was heels over head.

39.

I don't play soccer because I enjoy the sport. . . .

I'm just doing it for kicks.

40.

PEOPLE DON'T LIKE HAVING TO BEND OVER TO GET THEIR DRINKS.

We really need to raise the bar.

Were you there when the TV repairman got married?

The reception was excellent.

42.

DID YOU HEAR ABOUT THE DENTIST AND THE MANICURIST?

They fought tooth and nail.

43.

My doctor told me I had type A blood. . . .

But it was a Type-O.

44.

Why were the Indians here first?

They had reservations.

45.

If a seagull flies over the sea, what flies over the bay?

A bagel.

46.

What do you call a veterinarian with laryngitis?

A hoarse doctor.

47.

DID YOU HEAR ABOUT THE CANNIBAL WHO WAS LATE FOR DINNER?

He got the cold shoulder.

48.

How did Hitler tie his laces?

In little Nazis.

49.

Why do ambassadors never get sick?

Diplomatic immunity.

50.

What happens to deposed kings?

They get throne away.

51.

What kind of tree do fingers grow on?

A palm tree.

52.

WHAT DO YOU CALL A BABY MONKEY?

A chimp off the old block.

53.

What has four wheels and flies?

A garbage truck.

54.

WHAT DOES A SPY DO WHEN HE GETS COLD?

He goes undercover.

55.

What did the alien dandelion say to the Earth dandelion?

"Take me to your weeder!"

56.

Why did the little boy sleep on the chandelier?

Because he was a light sleeper.

57.

Why does lightning shock people?

Because it doesn't know how to conduct itself.

58.

What do prisoners use to call each other?

Cell phones.

59.

How do you tickle a rich girl?

Say, "Gucci, Gucci, Gucci!"

60.

Where did the king put his armies?

In his sleevies.

61.

WHY DON'T CANNIBALS EAT CLOWNS?

Because they taste funny.

62.

What is copper nitrate?

Overtime for policemen.

63.

How do crazy people go through the forest?

They take the psycho-path.

64.

WHAT DID THE COACH SAY TO HIS LOSING TEAM OF SNAKES?

"You can't venom all."

65.

How do you change tires on a duck?

With a quackerjack.

66.

What is a mouse's favorite game?

Hide and Squeak.

67.

What do you call a train loaded with toffee?

A chew chew train.

68.

When does a boat show affection?

When it hugs the shore.

69.

WHAT DO YOU CALL A FISH WITH NO EYES?

A fsh.

70.

Which president was least guilty?

Lincoln. He's in a cent.

71.

What do you call a rabbit with fleas?

Bugs Bunny.

72.

WHAT IS THE PURPOSE OF REINDEER?

It makes the grass grow, sweetie.

73.

What did the guitar say to the musician?

"Pick on someone your own size!"

74.

What do you call Santa's helpers?

Subordinate Clauses.

75.

WHAT DO YOU CALL TWO PEOPLE IN AN AMBULANCE?

A pair of medics.

76.

Why are rivers always rich?

Because they have two banks.

77.

What's the best time to go to the dentist?

Tooth hurty.

78.

What must you know to be an auctioneer?

Lots.

79.

What do you call a cow who gives no milk?

A milk dud.

80.

WHAT DID THE TOY STORE SIGN SAY?

"Don't feed the animals.
They are already stuffed."

81.

Did you hear about the dyslexic Satanist?

He sold his soul to Santa.

82.

What do you get when you drop a piano down a mineshaft?

A flat miner.

83.

Where did Noah keep his bees?

In the ark hives.

84.

HOW CAN A LEOPARD CHANGE HIS SPOTS?

By moving.

85.

Why are meteorologists always nervous?

Their future is always up in the air.

86.

**What do you call a dinosaur
with an extensive vocabulary?**

A thesaurus.

87.

**What is the difference between
one yard and two yards?**

A fence.

88.

**I DIDN'T LIKE MY BEARD
AT FIRST. . . .**

Then it grew on me.

89.

What do you get from a pampered cow?

Spoiled milk.

90.

Where do you find giant nails?

On the ends of giants' fingers.

91.

What's a three-season bed?

One without a spring.

92.

Why do cows wear cowbells?

Because their horns don't work.

93.

WHAT DISNEY MOVIE IS ABOUT A STUPID BOYFRIEND?

Dumb Beau.

94.

WHAT MUSICAL IS ABOUT A TRAIN CONDUCTOR?

"My Fare, Lady"

95.

I'm like the fabric version of King Midas. . . .

Everything I touch becomes felt.

96.

My wife first agreed to a date after I gave her a bottle of tonic water.

I Schwepped her off her feet.

97.

I always used to get small shocks when touching metal objects, but it recently stopped.

Needless to say, I'm ex-static.

98.

Why do Norwegians build their own tables?

No Ikea!

99.

Why did the coffee go to the police?

It got mugged.

100.

HOW MANY EARS DOES CAPTAIN KIRK HAVE?

Three: the left ear, the right ear, and the final frontier.

101.

I knew I shouldn't have had the seafood.

I'm feeling a little eel.

102.

**What's made of brass and
sounds like Tom Jones?**

Trombones.

103.

**What do you call an old person with really
good hearing?**

Deaf defying.

104.

MY WIFE KEEPS TELLING ME TO STOP PRETENDING TO BE BUTTER.

But I'm on a roll now.

105.

Why can't you be friends with a chipmunk?

They drive everyone nuts!

106.

I tried drag racing the other day.

It's murder trying to run in heels.

107.

HOW DOES DARTH VADER LIKE HIS TOAST?

On the dark side.

108.

A proud new dad sits down with his own father for a celebratory drink.

His father says, "Son, now you've got a child of your own, I think it's time you had this."

And with that, he pulls out a book called, "1001 Dad Jokes".

The new dad says, "Dad, I'm honored," as tears well up in his eyes.

His father says, "Hi Honored, I'm Dad."

109.

What kind of tea do you drink with the Queen?

Royal tea.

110.

My wife says she's leaving me because she thinks I'm too obsessed with astronomy.

What planet is she on!?

111.

I'm the Norse god of mischief but I don't like to talk about it.

I guess you could say I'm low-key.

112.

What do you call a woman who sounds like an ambulance?

Nina.

113.

THE CIRCLE IS JUST THE MOST RIDICULOUS SHAPE IN THE WORLD.

There's absolutely no point to it.

114.

There's been an explosion at a cheese factory in Paris.

There's nothing left but de brie.

115.

Last night, I had a dream that I was a muffler . . .

I woke up exhausted.

116.

WHAT ARE BALD SEA CAPTAINS MOST WORRIED ABOUT?

Cap sizes.

117.

No matter how kind you are . . .

German children are kinder.

118.

When is a cow hairy on the inside and the outside at the same time?

When it's standing in the doorway of the barn.

119.

WHAT DO YOU CALL A SNOWMAN WITH A SIX PACK?

An abdominal snowman.

120.

**After dinner, my wife asked me
if I could clear the table.**

I needed a run-up, but I made it.

121.

**Who was the roundest knight at King Arthur's
round table?**

Sir Cumference.

122.

AS I HANDED MY DAD HIS 50TH BIRTHDAY CARD, HE LOOKED AT ME WITH TEARS IN HIS EYES AND SAID . . .

"You know, one would have been enough."

123.

If prisoners could take their own mug shots, would they be called cellfies?

124.

Why do chicken coops only have two doors?

Because if they had four doors, they'd be chicken sedans.

125.

Where do you learn to make ice cream?

At sundae school.

126.

DOGS CAN'T OPERATE MRI MACHINES . . .

But catscan.

127.

I got an e-mail saying, "At Google Earth, we can read maps backwards!" and I thought . . .

"That's just spam."

128.

I can't stand stair lifts.

They drive me up the wall!

129.

How do you tell the difference between a frog and a horny toad?

A frog says, "Ribbit, Ribbit" and a horny toad says, "Rub it, Rub it".

130.

**My son must have been relieved
to have finally been born. . . .**

He looked like he was running out of womb in there.

131.

WHAT HAS TWO BUTTS AND KILLS PEOPLE?

An assassin.

132.

What do you call a cake baked by a hooker?

Hoe-made.

133.

My mom bought me a really cheap dictionary for my birthday.

I couldn't find the words to thank her.

134.

My friend and I started a new band and decided to call ourselves "Duvet" . . .

We only do covers.

135.

WHAT DO YOU CALL AN EXPLOSIVE HORSE?

Neigh-palm.

136.

**What type of magazines
do cows read?**

Cattlelogs.

137.

**A Dutchman has invented shoes that record
how many miles you've walked.**

Clever clogs.

138.

I tried to have a conversation with my wife when she was applying a mud pack.

You should have seen the filthy look she gave me.

139.

What do you call a horse that moves around a lot?

Unstable.

140.

I JUST TEXTED MY GIRLFRIEND RUTH AND TOLD HER THAT IT'S OVER BETWEEN US.

I'm Ruthless.

141.

One of the Russian acrobats in our human pyramid has been deported.

We don't have Oleg to stand on.

142.

WHY CAN'T A NOSE BE 12 INCHES LONG?

Because then it'd be a foot.

143.

Why does Piglet smell?

Because he plays with Pooh.

144.

Why did Mozart kill all his chickens?

Because when he asked them who the best composer was, they all said, "Bach, Bach, Bach."

145.

What is a ninja's favorite type of shoe?

Sneakers.

146.

Why do crabs never give to charity?

Because they're shellfish.

147.

How do astronomers organize a party?

They planet.

148.

How do you know when you're going to drown in milk?

When it's past your eyes.

149.

WHEN YOU HAVE A BLADDER INFECTION, URINE TROUBLE.

150.

OUR WEDDING WAS SO BEAUTIFUL . . .

even the cake was in tiers.

151.

What did one plate say to the other?

"Lunch is on me!"

152.

**Did you hear about the guy
who invented Lifesavers?**

They say he made a mint.

153.

How do you make anti-freeze?

Take away her blanket.

154.

WHAT DID THE BIG CHIMNEY SAY TO THE LITTLE CHIMNEY?

"You're too young to be smoking."

155.

What's the difference between bird flu and swine flu?

If you have bird flu, you need tweet-ment. If you have swine flu, you need oink-ment.

Why don't dinosaurs talk?

Because they're dead.

What does a martial arts expert drink?

Kara-tea.

158.

How do fish get high?

Seaweed.

159.

Why did Humpty Dumpty have a great fall?

To make up for an awful summer.

160.

WHY DO GHOSTS LOVE ELEVATORS?

Because they lift their spirits.

161.

What sound does a nut make when it sneezes?

"Cashew!"

162.

What did the tie say to the neck?

"I think I'll just hang around."

163.

What's a frog's favorite drink?

Croak-a Cola.

164.

What's a dentist's favorite musical instrument?

A tuba toothpaste.

165.

DID YOU HEAR ABOUT THAT NEW MOVIE CALLED CONSTIPATION?

No? That's because it's not out yet.

166.

What do you call a fly with no wings?

A walk.

167.

What do you call the security guards outside the Samsung factory?

The Guardians of the Galaxy.

168.

**What do you call a horse who
likes arts and crafts?**

A hobby horse.

169.

HOW DID THE HIPSTER BURN HIS MOUTH?

He drank his coffee before it
was cool.

170.

Who writes ghost stories?

A ghost writer.

171.

How do you catch a bra?

With a booby trap.

172.

HOW MANY LIVES DOES A GERMAN CAT HAVE?

Nein.

173.

What do you call a crab that plays baseball?

A pinch hitter.

174.

A devout Christian guy went to a remote island to work as a missionary but was captured by a tribe of cannibals who cooked and ate him.

He was very tender and tasty, but they were all violently sick afterwards.

It just goes to show that you can't keep a good man down.

175.

A hungry traveler stopped at a monastery and was taken to the kitchens where a brother is frying chips.

"Are you the friar?" he asked.

The brother replied, "No. I'm the chip monk."

176.

A DOCTOR HAD A REGULAR HABIT OF STOPPING OFF AT A BAR FOR A HAZELNUT DAIQUIRI ON HIS WAY HOME EVERY EVENING. **T**HE BARTENDER LEARNED HIS HABIT AND WOULD ALWAYS HAVE THE DRINK WAITING AT PRECISELY 5:03 P.M.

ONE AFTERNOON, AS FIVE O'CLOCK APPROACHED, THE BARTENDER WAS DISMAYED TO FIND THAT HE WAS OUT OF HAZELNUT EXTRACT.

THINKING QUICKLY, HE THREW TOGETHER A DAIQUIRI MADE WITH HICKORY NUTS AND SET IT ON THE BAR.

THE DOCTOR CAME IN AT HIS REGULAR TIME, TOOK ONE SIP OF THE DRINK, AND EXCLAIMED, "**T**HIS ISN'T A HAZELNUT DAIQUIRI!"

"**N**O, I'M SORRY," REPLIED THE BARTENDER, "IT'S A HICKORY DAIQUIRI, DOC."

177.

A guy goes to a psychiatrist and says, "Doc, I keep having these alternating, recurring dreams. First, I'm a teepee; then I'm a wigwam; then I'm a teepee; then I'm a wigwam. It's driving me crazy. What's wrong with me?"

The doctor replies, "It's very simple. You're two tents."

178.

Two boll weevils grew up in South Carolina. One went to Hollywood and, amazingly, became a famous actor. The other stayed behind in the cotton fields and never amounted to much.

The second one, naturally, became known as the lesser of two weevils.

179.

Did you hear about the Buddhist who refused Novocain during a root canal?

He wanted to transcend dental medication.

180.

Mahatma Gandhi, as everyone knows, walked barefoot most of the time, which produced an impressive set of calluses on his feet.

He also ate very little, which made him rather frail, and with his odd diet he suffered from bad breath.

This made him a super-calloused fragile mystic hexed by halitosis.

181.

A boy had a job bagging groceries at a supermarket. One day, the store installed a machine for squeezing fresh orange juice.

Intrigued, the young man eventually asked if he could be allowed to work the machine, but the store manager turned down his request, saying, "Sorry, kid, but baggers can't be juicers."

182.

What do a law student and a recovering alcoholic have in common?

They both have to pass the bar.

183.

Two Eskimos sitting in a kayak were chilly, so they lit a fire in the craft.

Unsurprisingly, it sank, proving once again that you can't have your kayak and heat it too.

184.

PEOPLE ARE USUALLY SHOCKED WHEN THEY FIND OUT I'M NOT A VERY GOOD ELECTRICIAN.

185.

Why do bears have heavy coats?

Fur protection.

186.

A SNAKE WALKS INTO A BAR.

The bartender asks, "How'd you do that?!"

187.

Marriage is grand.

Divorce is a hundred grand.

188.

My wife gave birth in the car on the way to the hospital.

She named him Carson.

189.

WHY CAN'T A MAN STARVE IN THE DESERT?

Because of all the
sand which is there.

190.

**I accidentally swallowed a
bunch of Scrabble tiles.**

My next trip to the bathroom could spell disaster.

191.

I have a steering wheel on my crotch.

It's driving me nuts.

192.

**To whoever stole my antidepressants,
I hope you're happy.**

193.

You can never run through campgrounds.

You can only ran, because it's past tents.

194.

What would you get if you stacked all the terrible dad jokes in a circle?

Groanhenge.

195.

AT WHAT TEMPERATURE DO THEY KEEP BLANKETS FOR NEWBORNS?

Womb temperature.

196.

Children in the dark make accidents.

But accidents in the dark make children.

197.

Someone sent me a video on WhatsApp saying, "I bet you can't watch this for more than 10 seconds!"

He was absolutely right . . . the video was only 5 seconds long.

198.

I HAVE A GOOD JOKE ABOUT TIME TRAVEL, BUT YOU DIDN'T LIKE IT.

199.

Two knights were fighting when one of them got their feet chopped off.

He was defeated.

200.

There's a really talented magician who speaks Spanish.

He goes to a party and says, "Alright, I'm going to disappear on the count of three: uno . . . dos . . ."

. . . and he was gone without a tres.

201.

I'm not addicted to brake fluid . . .

I can stop whenever I want.

202.

I HEARD A LITTLE PUN THE OTHER DAY.

It wasn't fully groan.

203.

**Why did the "A" go into the
bathroom and come out an "E"?**

He had a vowel movement.

204.

Why does Snoop Dogg carry an umbrella?

Fo' drizzle!

205.

Why don't dolphins ever make mistakes?

Everything they do is on porpoise!

206.

A COW WALKS INTO A POT FIELD.

The steaks have never been higher.

207.

**I'm sad I didn't get to see
how my execution ended. . . .**

I was left hanging.

208.

**Apparently, you can't use
"beefstew" as a password.**

It's not stroganoff.

209.

I thought swimming with the dolphins was expensive . . .

but swimming with the sharks cost me an arm and a leg!

210.

I BLINDFOLDED MY WIFE WITH A SCARF YESTERDAY.

I really pulled the wool over her eyes.

211.

I used to wonder where the sun went at night. . . .

Then it dawned on me.

212.

My wife burned her tongue drinking scalding hot coffee, and I thought of making a joke about it.

But then realized it would be in poor taste.

213.

I asked my daughter if she'd seen my newspaper. She told me that newspapers are old school. She said that people use tablets nowadays and handed me her iPad.

The fly didn't stand a chance. . . .

214.

Rumor has it that Uranus has a black hole in the center of it.

215.

SOME GERMAN CARS ARE VERY QUIET.

They are barely audi-ble.

216.

I don't like jokes about canned meat.

They're mostly spam.

217.

Have you heard of the new hipster weather forecasting device?

It lets you know when temperatures are dropping before anyone thinks they're cool.

218.

Want to hear a pizza joke?

Never mind, it's too cheesy.

219.

What do you call a fish with no legs?

A fish.

220.

A SHIPMENT OF VIAGRA HAS BEEN STOLEN

Police looking for
hardened criminals.

221.

You know the problem with grapes these days?

People just aren't raisin them right.

222.

SINGING IN THE SHOWER IS ALL FUN AND GAMES, UNTIL YOU GET SOAP IN YOUR MOUTH. . . .

Then it becomes a soap opera.

223.

What do you call a diced potato?

A squared root.

224.

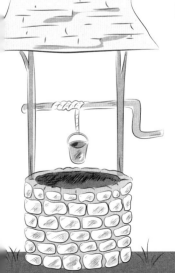

How do you know a wishing well works?

If your mother-in-law falls down it.

225.

WHAT ROOMS DO GHOSTS AVOID?

Living rooms.

226.

Man 1: Why did you buy a camouflage toilet seat?

Man 2: So my wife can't yell at me when I miss!

114

227.

What did the elephant say to the naked man?

"How do you breathe through that tiny trunk?"

228.

An amnesiac walks into a bar, goes up to a beautiful blonde, and says, "So, do I come here often?"

229.

Patient: "I was thinking about getting a vasectomy."

Doctor: "That's a big decision. Have you talked it over with your family?"

Patient: "Yes, we took a vote and they're in favor of it 17 to 2."

230.

A woman sees her husband standing on the bathroom scale, sucking in his stomach. "You know that's not going to help, right?" she asks.

"Sure it will," he says. "It's the only way I'll be able to see the numbers."

231.

SON: Dad, do you know the difference between a pack of cookies and a pack of elephants?
DAD: No.
SON: Then it's a good thing Mom does the grocery shopping!

232.

Son: Daddy, can I have a glass of water please?
Dad: I've given you six glasses of water already!
Son: Yes, but the backyard is still on fire!

233.

Why do dads take an extra pair of socks when they go golfing on Father's Day?

In case they get a hole in one!

234.

Dad: Son, if you keep pulling my hair, you will have to get off my shoulders.
Son: But, Dad, I'm just trying to get my gum back!

235.

Son: For $20, I'll be good.

Dad: Oh, yeah? When I was your age, I was good for nothing.

236.

WHAT DID THE FISH SAY WHEN HE HIT A CONCRETE WALL?

"Dam."

237.

A married couple was in a terrible accident where the woman's face was severely burned. The doctor told the husband that they couldn't graft any skin from her body because she was too skinny. So, the husband offered to donate some of his own skin. However, the only skin on his body that the doctor felt was suitable would have to come from his buttocks.

The husband and wife agreed that they would tell no one about where the skin came from and requested that the doctor also honor their secret. After all, this was a very delicate matter.

After the surgery was completed, everyone was astounded at the woman's new beauty. She looked more beautiful than she ever had before! All her friends and relatives just went on and on about her youthful beauty!

One day, she was alone with her husband, and she was overcome with emotion at his sacrifice. She said, "Dear, I just want to thank you for everything you did for me. There is no way I could ever repay you."

"My darling," he replied, "think nothing of it. I get all the thanks I need every time I see your mother kiss you on the cheek."

238.

WHAT DO ESKIMOS GET FROM SITTING ON THE ICE TOO LONG?

Polaroids.

239.

How do you get holy water?

Boil the hell out of it.

240.

What do the letters D.N.A. stand for?

National Dyslexic Association.

241.

What do you get when you cross a snowman with a vampire?

Frostbite.

242.

What has four legs, is big, green, and fuzzy, and if it fell out of a tree would kill you?

A pool table.

243.

**Why are there so many
Smiths in the phone book?**

They all have phones.

244.

WHAT DO YOU CALL A HIPPIE'S WIFE?

Mississippi.

245.

What do you get when you cross a pit bull with a collie?

A dog that runs for help after it bites your leg off.

246.

What does it mean when the flag is at half-mast at the post office?

They're hiring.

247.

I DREAMED I WAS DROWNING IN AN OCEAN OF ORANGE SODA LAST NIGHT.

It took me a while to work out that it was just a Fanta sea.

248.

At work we have a printer that we named Bob Marley.

It's always jammin'.

249.

I've decided Hershey's chocolate is too feminist for my taste.

I'm switching to Hishey's.

250.

Why do bagpipers walk when they play?

They're trying to get away from the noise.

127

251.

I start a new job in Seoul next week.

I hope it's going to be a good Korea move.

252.

DO I ENJOY MAKING COURTHOUSE PUNS?

Guilty.

253.

What do you call a sketchy Italian neighborhood?

The spaghetto.

254.

I got caught stealing a leg of lamb from the supermarket.
The security guard said, "What do you think you're doing with that?"
I replied, "Potatoes, peas, and gravy would be nice."

255.

I CAN'T DECIDE IF I WANT TO PURSUE A CAREER AS A WRITER OR A GRIFTER.

I'm still weighing the prose and cons.

256.

I don't often tell dad jokes,
but when I do, he laughs.

257.

A man walks into a bookstore and asks,
"Can I have a book by Shakespeare?"
"Of course, sir, which one?"
"William."

258.

**Accordion to a recent survey, inserting
musical instruments into sentences
largely goes unnoticed.**

259.

I don't know why Marvel hasn't tried to put advertisements on the Hulk.

He's essentially a giant Banner.

260.

I'll never date another apostrophe.

The last one was too possessive.

261.

WHAT DO YOU CALL A ROW OF PEOPLE LIFTING MOZZARELLA?

A cheesy pick up line.

262.

What's Donald Trump's favorite brand of gum?

Bigly chew.

263.

WHY CAN'T YOU EAT WOOKIE MEAT?

Because it's too Chewy.

264.

People tell me the story of Jesus is made up. . . .

But I think it Israel.

265.

A grasshopper walks into a bar. The bartender says, "I'm going to serve you a drink named after you."

The grasshopper replies, "You have a drink named Steve?!"

266.

I gave all my dead batteries away, free of charge.

267.

**What would _Rocky_ be called
if it was a hockey movie?**

Rockey.

268.

I dig, you dig, we dig, she digs, he digs, they dig.

It's not a beautiful poem, but it's very deep.

269.

Dad: "You know how scuba divers sit on the edge of the boat and fall out backwards into the water? You know why they do that?"

Son: "No, why?"

Dad: "If they went forward they'd fall into the boat!"

270.

IT'S REALLY HARD TO SAY WHAT MY WIFE DOES FOR A LIVING.

She sells sea shells by the sea shore.

271.

I just swapped our bed for a trampoline.

My wife hit the roof.

272.

TODAY, MY SON ASKED, "CAN I HAVE A BOOKMARK?" AND I BURST INTO TEARS. . . .

11 years old and he still doesn't know my name is Brian.

138

273.

My wife is really mad at the fact that I have no sense of direction.

So I packed up my stuff and right.

274.

DAD: I was just listening to the radio on my way into town. Apparently an actress just killed herself.

MOM: Oh my! Who!?

DAD: Uh, I can't remember. . . . I think her name was Reese something?

MOM: WITHERSPOON?!

DAD: No, it was with a knife. . . .

275.

I bought some shoes from a drug dealer.

I don't know what he laced them with, but I was tripping all day!

276.

Did you know the first french fries weren't actually cooked in France?

They were cooked in Greece.

278.

IF A CHILD REFUSES TO SLEEP DURING NAP TIME, ARE THEY GUILTY OF RESISTING A REST?

279.

The secret service isn't allowed to yell "Get down!" anymore when the president is about to be attacked.

Now they have to yell, "Donald, duck!"

280.

I'M READING A BOOK ABOUT ANTI-GRAVITY.

It's impossible to put down!

281.

What do you call someone with no body and no nose?

Nobody knows.

282.

A slice of apple pie is $2.50 in Jamaica and $3.00 in the Bahamas.

These are the pie rates of the Caribbean.

283.

What is the least spoken language in the world?

Sign language.

284.

My daughter screeched, "Daaaaaad, you haven't listened to one word I've said, have you!?"

What a strange way to start a conversation with me. . . .

285.

I ORDERED A CHICKEN AND AN EGG FROM AMAZON . . . I'LL LET YOU KNOW.

286.

My wife tried to unlatch our daughter's car seat with one hand and asked, "How do one-armed mothers do it?"

Without missing a beat, I replied, "Single handedly."

287.

My friend keeps saying "Cheer up, man, it could be worse. You could be stuck underground in a hole full of water."

I know he means well.

288.

Justice is a dish best served cold.

If it were served warm it would be justwater.

289.

MOM: "How do I look?"
DAD: "With your eyes."

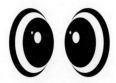

290.

Spring is here! I got so excited I wet my plants!

291.

3 UNWRITTEN
RULES OF LIFE:

1.
2.
3.

292.

IF YOU SEE A ROBBERY AT AN APPLE STORE DOES THAT MAKE YOU AN iWITNESS?

293.

Did you hear that FedEx and UPS are merging?

They're going to go by the name Fed-Up from now on.

294.

Don't trust atoms.
They make up everything!

295.

I told my son I was named after
Thomas Jefferson . . . He said,
"But Dad, your name is Brian."

I said, "I know, but I was named AFTER
Thomas Jefferson."

296.

KID: "Dad, make me a sandwich!"
DAD: "Poof, you're a sandwich!"

297.

Why did the invisible man turn down the job offer?

He couldn't see himself doing it.

298.

SERVER: "Sorry about your wait."

DAD: "Are you saying I'm fat?"

299.

WHAT'S THE BEST PART ABOUT LIVING IN SWITZERLAND?

I don't know, but the flag is a big plus.

300.

If Snoop Dogg dies before pot becomes legal in the US, he will be rolling in his grave.

301.

WHAT DO YOU CALL A DOG THAT CAN DO MAGIC?

A Labracadabrador.

302.

What do you call a deer with no eyes?

No idea!

303.

GRANDPA: I have a "dad bod."
DAD: To me it's more like a father figure.

304.

WHAT'S FORREST GUMP'S PASSWORD?

1forrest1.

305.

I used to have a job at a calendar factory . . .

but I got the sack because I took a couple of days off.

306.

Why didn't the vampire attack Taylor Swift?

She had bad blood.

307.

Why did Santa go to college for music?

So he could improve his wrapping skills.

308.

I asked the lion in the wardrobe what he was doing there . . .

He said it was Narnia business!

309.

Did you hear about the dog who gave birth on the side of the road?

She was ticketed for littering.

156

310.

A SHEEP, A DRUM, AND A SNAKE FALL OVER A CLIFF . . .

Ba-Dum-Tss.

311.

Man: Waiter, this coffee tastes like mud!

Waiter: Yes sir, it is fresh ground.

312.

I used to be a banker . . .

But then I lost interest.

313.

WHY DID ADELE CROSS THE ROAD?

To say hello from the other side.

314.

I should have been sad when my flashlight batteries died. . . .

But I was delighted.

315.

Why isn't Cinderella good at soccer?

Because her coach is a pumpkin and she keeps running away from the ball!

316.

SOMEONE THREW A BOTTLE OF OMEGA-3 PILLS AT ME.

Luckily, my injuries were only super fish oil.

317.

A guitarist passed out on stage.

He must have rocked himself to sleep.

318.

Did you hear about the important pickle?

It was a big dill!

319.

Why can't you give Elsa a balloon?

Because she'll let it go.

320.

Why don't you iron a four-leaf clover?

Because you don't want to press your luck.

321.

How much room is needed for fungi to grow?

As mushroom as possible!

322.

WHY DOES WALDO ALWAYS WEAR STRIPES?

Because he doesn't want to be spotted.

323.

Tried to catch fog yesterday. . . .

Mist.

324.

**I have a lot of jokes about
unemployed people . . .**

but none of them work.

325.

WHEN CHEMISTS DIE, THEY BARIUM.

326.

Jokes about German sausage are the würst.

327.

**I took a class trip to the
Coca-Cola Museum.**

I hope there's no pop quiz.

328.

How does Moses make his tea?

Hebrews it.

329.

This girl said she recognized me from the vegetarian club, but I'd never met herbivore.

330.

I did a theatrical performance about puns.

It was a play on words.

331.

PMS JOKES AREN'T FUNNY, PERIOD.

332.

What do you call a soldier who survived mustard gas and pepper spray?

A seasoned veteran.

333.

ENERGIZER BUNNY ARRESTED.
CHARGED WITH BATTERY.

335.

Did you hear the joke about the dry erase board?

It's remarkable!

334.

**I got a job at a bakery because
I kneaded the dough.**

336.

**England has no kidney bank,
but it does have a Liverpool.**

337.

**I dropped out of Communism class
because of lousy Marx.**

338.

All the toilets in New York City's police stations have been stolen. Police have nothing to go on.

339.

What does a clock do when it's hungry?

Go back four seconds.

340.

**Haunted French pancakes
give me the crèpes.**

341.

**I wondered why the baseball
was getting bigger. . . .**

Then it hit me!

342.

Cartoonist found dead in home.
Details are sketchy.

343.

Venison for dinner?

Oh deer!

344.

I USED TO THINK I WAS INDECISIVE, BUT NOW I'M NOT SO SURE. . . .

345.

Be kind to your dentist.

He has fillings too.

346.

What do you call a potato wearing sunglasses?

A spectater.

347.

Dad: There's going to be thousands
of people in Bristol tonight.
Son: Why?
Dad: Because they live there!

348.

HOW DOES THE MAN ON THE MOON GET HIS HAIR CUT?

Eclipse it.

349.

Brother: What would you do if I fell down a cliff?
Sister: I'd call you an ambulance, of course!
Dad: How would that help? He's at the bottom of a cliff dying, and you're shouting, "YOU'RE AN AMBULANCE!"

350.

How do you hide an elephant?

You paint it red! Have you ever seen
a red elephant? I didn't think so!

351.

Dad: What comes after
S in the alphabet?
Daughter: T?
Dad: I'll have milk
and two sugars,
thanks!

177

352.

**Why isn't dark spelled with a
"c" instead of a "k?"**

Because you can't see in the dark!

353.

WHY DOES ED SHEERAN
NOT HAVE A GIRLFRIEND?

Because Sheeran away.

354.

**Two years ago, my doctor told me
I was going deaf.**

I haven't heard from him since.

355.

**Remember when air for your tires
was free and now it's $1.50?**

It's because of inflation.

356.

What will a dad say if you ask him if he's alright?

"No, I'm half left."

Son: Hey, I was thinking . . .
Dad: I thought I smelled something burning!

358.

TWO GUYS WALK INTO A BAR, BUT THE THIRD ONE DUCKS.

359.

**How many tickles does it take
to make an octopus laugh?**

Ten-tickles.

360.

WHEN A WOMAN IS GIVING BIRTH, SHE IS LITERALLY KIDDING.

361.

A ham sandwich walks into a bar and orders a beer. The bartender says, "Sorry, we don't serve food here."

362.

A string walks into a bar with a few friends and orders a beer. The bartender says, "I'm sorry, but we don't serve strings here."

The string goes back to his table. He ties himself in a loop and messes up the top of his hair. He walks back up to the bar and orders a beer. The bartender squints at him and says, "Hey, aren't you a string?"

The string says, "Nope, I'm a frayed knot."

363.

Can February March?

No, but April May!

364.

WHAT DID THE BUFFALO SAY TO HIS SON WHEN HE DROPPED HIM OFF AT SCHOOL?

"Bison."

365.

Two peanuts were walking down the street.
One was a salted.

184

366.

What do you call a cow with two legs?

Lean beef.

367.

What do you call a cow with no legs?

Ground beef.

368.

What do you call a dead fly?

A flew.

369.

What is Beethoven's favorite fruit?

A ba-na-na-na.

370.

Where did the college-aged vampire like to shop?

Forever 21.

371.

CASHIER: "Paper or plastic?"
DAD: "Either, I'm bisacktual."

372.

WHAT DID THE HORSE SAY AFTER IT TRIPPED?

"Help! I've fallen and I can't giddyup!"

373.

You know what the loudest pet you can get is?

A trumpet.

374.

What noise does a 747 make when it bounces?

"Boeing, Boeing, Boeing."

**I hear it's easy to get ladies
not to eat Tide pods.**

It's more difficult to deter gents, though.

376.

WHAT DO YOU CALL A FACTORY THAT MAKES PASSABLE PRODUCTS?

A satisfactory.

377.

Waitress: "Soup or salad?"
Dad: "I don't want a SUPER salad,
I want a regular salad."

378.

Did you hear about the circus fire?

It was in tents!

379.

You're American when you go into the bathroom, and you're American when you come out, but do you know what you are while you're in there?

European.

380.

**I'm only familiar with 25 letters
in the English language.**

I don't know why.

381.

**A woman is on trial for beating her husband
to death with his guitar collection. The
judge asks, "First offender?"**

She says, "No, first a Gibson! Then a Fender!"

382.

WHAT DOES AN ANGRY PEPPER DO?

It gets jalapeño your face.

383.

What does a nosy pepper do?

It gets jalapeño business.

384.

As a lumberjack, I know that I've cut exactly 2,417 trees. I know because every time I cut one, I keep a log.

385.

Did you hear the one about the bed?

No? That's because it hasn't been made up yet!

386.

**What do you get when you cross
an elephant with a rhino?**

Elephino.

387.

I WAS INTERROGATED OVER THE THEFT OF A CHEESE TOASTIE.

Man, they really grilled me.

388.

**What happens if you rearrange
the letters of "Postmen?"**

They get really pissed off!

389.

**Did you see they made round bales of hay
illegal in Wisconsin?**

It's because the cows weren't getting a square meal.

390.

WHAT DO YOU CALL A LONELY CHEESE?

Provolone.

391.

Dad (to a singer): Don't forget a bucket.

Singer: Why?

Dad: To carry your tune.

392.

I told my 14-year-old son I thought "Fortnite" was a stupid name for a computer game . . . I think it is just too weak.

393.

How do you make a Kleenex dance?

Put a little boogie in it!

394.

WHY DID THE FARMER GIVE THE PONY A GLASS OF WATER?

Because he was a little horse!

395.

Nurse: "Blood type?"
Dad: "Red."

396.

I heard Youtube, Twitter, and Facebook are all merging. They're going to call it You-Twit-Face.

397.

I tried to get reservations to the library, but they were completely booked!

398.

A TERMITE WALKS INTO A BAR AND ASKS, "IS THE BAR TENDER HERE?"

399.

How do you find Will Smith in the snow?

You look for fresh prints.

400.

Studies show that cows produce more milk when farmers talk to them.

It's a case of in one ear and out the udder.

401.

THE INVENTOR OF THE THROAT LOZENGE HAS DIED.

There will be no coffin at his funeral.

202

402.

Why aren't Greeks morning people?

Because Dawn is tough on grease.

403.

Why did the cowboy get a dachshund?

Someone told him to get a long little doggie.

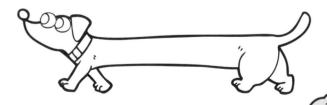